The Learning Works

Create a M

A Complete Framework for Students to Use in Creating an Original Magazine

Grades 5–8

Written by Delana S. Heidrich
Illustrated by Bev Armstrong • Cover Art by Lucyna A. M. Green

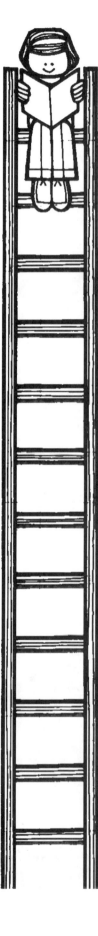

The Learning Works

Editing and Text Design:
Clark Editorial & Design

The purchase of this book entitles the individual teacher to reproduce copies for use in the classroom. The reproduction of any part for an entire school or school system or for commercial use is strictly prohibited. No form of this work may be reproduced, transmitted, or recorded without written permission from the publisher. Inquiries should be addressed to the Permissions Department.

Copyright © 1999
The Learning Works, Inc.
Santa Barbara, California 93160

ISBN: 0-88160-310-4
LW 379

Printed in the United States of America.

Contents

Introduction 5–6

Section I • First Things First

Selecting a Theme 8
Selecting a Title 9
Selecting a Filing System 10
Assigning Duties 11
Recording Your Decisions 12

Section II • Getting Down to the Business of Writing

The Production of a Magazine 14
A Word from the Editor 15–17
Contributors' Corner: Introducing Your Group Members 18–20
The Mailbox: Letters from Readers 21–23
Special Report 24–26
Profiles and Interviews 27–29
Poetry and Short Stories 30–32
New Products Preview 33–35
"A Look Back" or "Future Forward" 36–38
How-To's: Writing Instructions 39–41
Voice of the Critic: Recommending Events and Activities 42–44
Advice Column: Writing Questions and Answers 45–47
What's New?: Reporting on the News, Sports, and Entertainment 48–50
Essays and Opinions 51–53
Keeping Track 54

Table of Contents
(continued)

Section III • Creating Your Magazine

Designing the Front Cover	56
Adding the Ads	57–58
It's the "In" Thing: Adding Fashion Pages	59–60
Adding Some Fun: Cartoons, Jokes, Puzzles, and Games	61–62
Designing the Back Cover	63
Putting It All Together: Placing Articles, Ads, and Extras	64
Recording Your Decisions	65
Packaging Your Product	66

Section IV • Evaluating Your Work

Trading Magazines	68
Evaluation Form	69–70
Conducting a Discussion Group	71
Discussion Group Questions	72
Revision Decisions	73–74

Section V • Sharing Your Creation

Inviting Guests to the Magazine Trade Show	76–77
Setting up Your Magazine Display Booth	78
Producing a Televised, Live, or Radio Broadcast Magazine Show	79–83
Presenting, Reading, and Demonstrating Article Information	84
Specified Duties	85
Product Evaluation Form	86
Making the Most of Your Magazine Experience	87
Proofreader's Marks	88

Introduction

Create a Magazine is a complete language arts unit that requires students to write profiles, interviews, journalistic reports, short stories, letters, instructions, and critical reviews. In addition to perfecting writing styles, students also practice working in cooperative groups, organizing information according to a central theme, and displaying, demonstrating, and presenting ideas to others.

Create a Magazine is divided into five sections:
- First Things First
- Getting Down to the Business of Writing
- Creating Your Magazine
- Evaluating Your Work
- Sharing Your Creation

Section I • First Things First

This section allows cooperative groups to decide on their magazine's theme and title, create a filing system to organize their work, and assign duties to group members. There are two possible approaches to assigning duties. Students may decide which group members will be responsible for the writing of the various magazine articles, or each student can write a version of all the articles. In the latter case, groups can rate each other's writings to determine which articles and other items will be included in the final magazine.

Section II • Getting Down to the Business of Writing

These activities introduce students to various writing styles and requires them to practice and perfect their skills with each. Depending on whether you decide to have each student write a version of each article, or groups divide writing duties among their members, the magazine project can be completed in four to eight weeks.

Introduction
(continued)

Section III • Creating Your Magazine

This section provides guidelines for cooperative groups on how to structure their magazines. It includes suggestions on such topics as determining the placement of articles; creating an index page; adding advertisements, cartoons, and puzzle pages; designing the magazine's front and back covers; and packaging the magazine in a workable folder or binder.

Section IV • Evaluating Your Work

These activities encourage students to critique their own work and the work of others, and to make recommended revisions before their final projects are displayed to a larger audience.

Section V • Sharing Your Creation

This selection of culminating activities offers unique ideas for the presentation of magazines at a Magazine Trade Show where students attempt to "sell" their pilot magazines to publishers and consumers. In presenting their magazines, students are encouraged to create audio and video displays, booth backdrops, dramatizations, and other exciting presentation props and performances.

Note: Encourage students to videotape or photograph their group members at work on their magazines. These images can be displayed at the Magazine Trade Show as part of the students' multimedia presentations.

Section I
First Things First

First Things First   Name _____

Selecting a Theme

Glance at a magazine rack in a supermarket, bookstore, or newsstand. The subject areas covered by magazine publishers are nearly limitless—from animals to animation, from bicycles to business, from humor to history. You can find a magazine devoted to the coverage of just about every topic or interest.

During the next several weeks, you and your group members will be working to create your own *pilot* magazine. A pilot is the first issue of a magazine—a trial run. At the end of this unit, you will exhibit your pilot magazine at a Magazine Trade Show. Your pilot magazine should be well written, exciting, informative, and fun. It also must have a theme that you and your group members will be excited to work with over the next several weeks. Your group may choose to write a magazine about sports, entertainment, music, or technology—whatever interests you. When choosing a theme, keep in mind that all of your writings will carry that theme, so choose something versatile and exciting.

On the lines below, write six possible themes for your group's magazine.

_____   _____

_____   _____

_____   _____

Now take a vote and record your group's final decision here.

_____

First Things First   Name _____

Selecting a Title

Once you and your fellow group members have decided on a theme for your pilot magazine, you will need to decide on a title that is short, catchy, and appropriate for your magazine's subject area. Magazine titles seldom exceed two or three words. They are intended to capture the essence of the magazine's overall theme. They are general enough to fit not only the stories covered in the current issue, but those planned for future issues as well. Deciding on a title now—before you begin writing your magazine—will help you define your audience and narrow your article topics.

On the lines below, list some actual magazine titles and the theme or subject area each magazine covers. The first one has been done for you.

Magazine Title	Magazine Theme
Time	news and social issues of our times
_____	_____
_____	_____
_____	_____

On the lines below, write six titles that would fit the theme of your magazine.

_____   _____
_____   _____
_____   _____

Vote on a title for your group's magazine and record the winning title here.

_____

9

Create a Magazine
© The Learning Works, Inc.

First Things First   Name _____

Selecting a Filing System

How wonderful it would be if all you had to do in school during the next two months was work on your magazine! Alas, there are still book reports and unit tests, worksheets and warm-ups all demanding your attention. So, you and your other group members will need an organizational system and a place to keep your works-in-progress until your magazine is completed.

The organization of your papers will require at least two manila folders or 10 x 13 mailing envelopes with your group's magazine title written on the covers. Choose a filing system that works for all of the members of your group and meets with your teacher's approval.

System 1: "Complete" and "Incomplete" Folders

Your group may choose to use two folders or mailing envelopes that will be stored in the same location in the classroom every day. The first folder will be labeled with the name of your group's magazine and the words "Incomplete Works," and the second with your magazine's name and the words "Completed Works." As members complete articles, ads, and stories, they will move them from the "Incomplete" to the "Completed" file.

System 2: Section Folders

Rather than having a general Completed and Incomplete folder, your group may choose to create folders that store information related to each magazine section. Thus, folders would be labeled with the name of your group's magazine and such titles as "Letters to the Editor" and "Advertisements." You will need an additional folder labeled "Completed Works" in which you will store finished pieces. The advantage of this system is that all papers pertaining to any one section can be easily located when it is time to work on your magazine.

System 3: Student Folders

Instead of storing incomplete works in folders labeled with article titles, you may store them in folders labeled with the names of students in your group. The advantage of this approach is that each student working on his or her own specific areas of the magazine may store information in his or her own folder. When it is time to work as a group, each student simply pulls his or her own file. This approach also simplifies things if you choose to work on your magazine at home, since you do not need to take home the entire "Incomplete" folder or several section folders, but only your personal folder. Be sure the name of your group's magazine is written on each folder, that all folders are stored in the same place in the classroom each day, and that you have a "Completed Works" folder for completed articles.

Our group chooses the _____ filing system.

First Things First

Assigning Duties

The creation of a pilot magazine will require the full effort of each member of your group. Your teacher may want each student in your group to write his or her own version of all of the items (although only one version of each item will make it into the final magazine), or your teacher may allow you to decide within your group who will be responsible for writing individual items. *In either case, each group member must contribute at least two items to your group's final magazine.*

If each student writes a separate version of each magazine item, other groups can help you decide which items to include in your group's final magazine. Have all of your group members who are interested in submitting an item to the final magazine remove their names from their papers and hand them to another group. The other group will rate competing pieces, and the one with the highest rating will be included in your magazine. Once you have had two items accepted, wait until all other group members have also had two items accepted before submitting additional items for consideration. Use the following criteria for rating the items given to you by another group. Rate each item on a scale from 1 to 10 with 10 being the highest score.

This item is organized logically and written clearly. (1–10) _____

This item has few mechanical or grammatical errors. (1–10) _____

The subject matter is interesting. (1–10) _____

This item fulfills the requirements of its category. (1–10) _____

This item is laid out effectively. (1–10) _____

Final rating (total all ratings above) _____

First Things First   Name _____

Recording Your Decisions

The members of our group are: _____
_____
_____

Our magazine's title is: _____
Our magazine's theme or subject is: _____
We will use the following filing system: _____

Magazine Task	Responsible Party or Parties
A Word from the Editor	all group members
Contributors' Corner	all group members
The Mailbox	_____
The Special Report	_____
The Profile or Interview	_____
The Short Story or Poetry	_____
New Products Preview	_____
"A Look Back" or "Future Forward"	_____
The How-To	_____
The Critical Review	_____
Advice Column	all group members
What's New?	_____
Essay/Opinion Page	_____
The Advertisements	_____
The Fun Pages	_____
The Index	_____
The Front Cover	_____
The Back Cover	_____

Create a Magazine
© The Learning Works, Inc.

The Production of a Magazine

Writing articles is only one step in the process of publishing a magazine. Copy editors, proofreaders, graphic artists, and others all contribute their efforts to produce a professional-looking product. You and the other members of your group can do the same. Begin by reading the ideas below.

Writing Effective Headlines

1. Write a story's headline *after* writing the story itself so you will have lots of details to refer to in creating the most effective title.

2. Create catchy titles that highlight some aspect of the story, but require that the reader read on to make complete sense of the headline.

3. Keep headlines *short*. Brief phrases are more effective attention-getters than long, complete sentences.

Proofreading Each Other's First Drafts

To simplify proofreading and its interpretation, stick to the use of standard correction symbols. A list of proofreader's marks and their meanings appears on page 88 of this book.

Laying Out Your Stories

This task can be made much easier by using a computer. If a computer is not available, final-draft articles can be completed on a typewriter. Either way, follow these hints in laying out your stories.

1. Maintain plenty of white space on every page. A page completely covered in words is not as easy to read as one that looks clean and uncluttered.

2. Stick to a single type style (font) and size (usually 10 or 12 points) for the body of all articles. Use black print on white paper for the body of all articles.

3. Experiment with various font styles and sizes, colors, italics, capital letters, bold, and underlining to add style to headlines, advertisements, puzzles, cartoons, and other areas of the magazine that are not the body of core articles.

4. Add clip art, student artwork, graphs, charts, photocopied photographs, and other extras throughout your magazine.

5. Experiment with different story formats. For example, you might want to lay out longer stories in two or three columns.

A Word from the Editor

The editorial in a magazine is a *first-person essay* written in a *conversational tone* by the magazine's editor addressing some topic or theme covered in a specific issue of the magazine. Since your magazine is a pilot issue, your editorial will explain why your group felt it was important to create this new magazine.

Your editorial's **introduction** should consist of an interesting quote or anecdote or some other quick attention-getter. The **body** of your editorial should explain why your magazine is needed, how it differs from other magazines on the market, and what columns and features it will carry. The **conclusion** of your editorial should contain an upbeat sales pitch and should thank your audience for their interest in your publication.

All group members should work together to write the editorial page for your magazine since it will set the tone for your entire project. The worksheet and writing steps on page 16 and the sample on page 17 will help you get started.

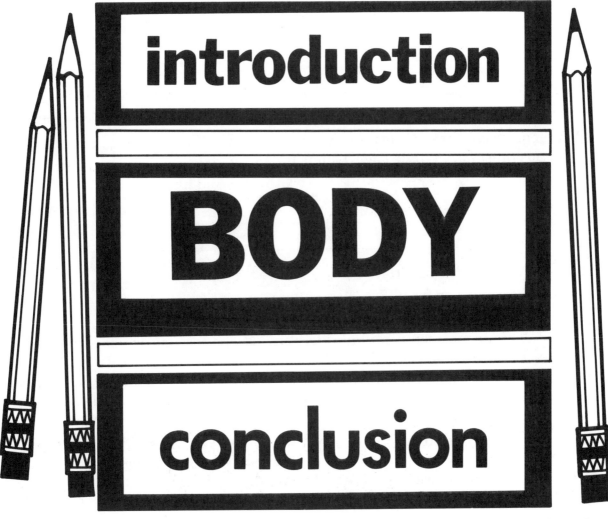

Getting Down to the Business of Writing   Name _____

Editorial Worksheet

1. Locate and record at least three quotes that might be used in your editorial's introduction. The quotes can be taken from newspapers, magazines, books, calendars, bumper stickers, etc., but they must pertain to your magazine's overall theme. (Remember to credit the source of any quotes you use.)

   _____
   _____
   _____

2. Give three possible reasons your magazine is needed on the market (e.g., takes a new approach to a familiar topic, covers a relatively uncovered topic)

   _____
   _____
   _____

3. List three ways your magazine will differ from other magazines covering your topic.

   _____
   _____
   _____

4. List regular columns and features your magazine will contain (e.g., Profiles of Famous Musicians, Puzzle Page, Letters from Readers)

   _____
   _____
   _____

Steps for Writing the Editorial
1. Study the sample on page 17.
2. Decide on a title for your editorial page.
3. Have all group members contribute ideas and use the answers on this worksheet to create a clear, complete, and effective column. Elect a secretary to record a first draft of your editorial page.
4. Ask members of another group to help you proof your first draft for both content clarity and grammatical errors.
5. Use the layout tips on page 14 to help you prepare a professional-looking final draft of your editorial. Store the finished document in your "Completed Works" folder until you are ready to place it in your final magazine.

Getting Down to the Business of Writing

A Word from the Editor

Dear Reader,

interesting anecdote

A few years ago I had lunch with a photojournalist friend of mine. He had just returned from Bosnia where he recorded in photographs a civil war that he believed could not be described in words alone. My friend was frustrated because when he returned home, his local newspaper did not wish to cover the important Bosnia story.

So many events happen around the globe in a given day that it is difficult for newspapers to choose what to cover in their limited pages. After listening to my friend's story, I became curious about just how those choices are made. So I began to dig for the stories behind the stories, and what I learned was intriguing. Politics, personality, and marketability all play into decisions about what you read in the paper and watch on the evening news.

why magazine needed on market

The News Behind the News is a new magazine dedicated to bringing you the story behind the story. We will tell you how the front-page story made it to the front page, why the back-page story didn't, and explore some of the stories you weren't meant to read at all. Through interviews, personal profiles, book reviews, and more we will introduce you to the makers and the breakers of news stories as well as to the people who are the stories.

columns and features

how magazine differs

Unlike other news magazines, we are committed to honesty and openness. The only reason we will ever omit a story is because we have run out of pages. Politics, personal biases, and unfavorable marketability predictions will not stop us from breaking the news or the news behind the news.

sales pitch and thank-you

We created *The News Behind the News* because there is always more to the story—or the absence of a story—than the other news magazines will let you know about. We are committed to bringing you the rest of the story, and we thank you for reading all about it.

Sincerely,

The Editor

THE NEWS Behind THE NEWS

Contributors' Corner: Introducing Your Group Members

Magazines sometimes include a page of information about authors of some of the articles in a current issue. The "Contributors' Corner" is intended to introduce readers to both staff writers and free-lance authors who contributed to the magazine. The biographical sketches list professional titles and/or experiences that qualify the authors to write the articles they have written, list other articles and/or books the authors have written, and highlight a few details from the personal life of each author. An author biography seldom exceeds a paragraph in length.

Your magazine will contain a page that will introduce your group members. Each group member will write a single paragraph emphasizing interests and skills that qualify him or her to write about the themes covered in your magazine and indicating what parts of the magazine he or she worked on. These biographical sketches may also list other works the author has written including book reports, essays, and other class assignments.

Complete the worksheet and follow the steps on the next page in writing your own biographical sketch. Then work with your group to decide how your individual paragraphs will be arranged to produce a professional-looking "Contributors' Corner" page for your final magazine. A sample "Contributor's Corner" appears on page 20.

Getting Down to the Business of Writing

Contributors' Corner Worksheet

1. Tell why you are interested in the topic of your magazine _____
   _____

2. List special skills that qualify you to write about your magazine's subject area.
   _____
   _____

3. Record a few interesting things about your personal life, including sports or clubs you are involved in, hobbies, family members, pets, etc.
   _____
   _____

4. List other things you have written, including essays, reports, and even letters.
   _____
   _____

Steps for Writing the Contributors' Corner Page

1. Using the information you recorded above and referring to the sample paragraphs on the following page, write a four- to six-sentence biographical sketch in *third person* highlighting your qualifications for contributing to your group's magazine.
2. Share your paragraph with the other members of your group so you can work together to revise each other's first drafts.
3. Write a revised draft of your biographical sketch.
4. Decide with your other group members how to arrange all of the paragraphs on one or two pages, and elect a group member to either cut and paste individual paragraphs or retype the paragraphs to create a "Contributors' Corner." Add student self-portraits or photographs, if you like.

Create a Magazine
© The Learning Works, Inc.

Contributors' Corner

 Matt Baker has been a fan of rock music since his ninth birthday when his father gave him an Elvis Presley CD. He is a senior staff writer for *Modern Music* and author of the "What's New?" column. Matt is the author of "Matilda: A Book Report," and "Rocks!" an earth science essay. In this issue, Matt reports on a new wave in the world of jazz.

 Candy Simms is a free-lance writer and regular contributor to *Modern Music*. She plays trumpet for the Butte City Middle School Band. This month Candy contributes a profile of BCMS band conductor, Thomas Raye. She is a prolific writer of short stories and poems about music and the arts.

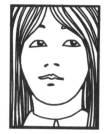 Kim Kelly is the lead writer for our "New Products Preview" column. This month, Kim reviews Electro City's latest compact disc player and Stix Unlimited's newest drum set. Her story, "All Alone," earned her an "A" in Ms. Jones' English class.

 Tom Scott sings in the Butte City Middle School choir and regularly writes poems in Ms. Jones' English class. His essay on "Music of the Future" can be found on page 11 of this issue of *Modern Music*.

Getting Down to the Business of Writing

The Mailbox: Letters from Readers

Many magazines publish letters they receive from readers. Depending on the theme of the magazine, letters that are published may be readers' responses to articles published in the previous issue, as well as readers' theme-related tips, advice, and suggestions. News magazines, for example, typically publish readers' editorial comments on articles in the previous issue, while parenting magazines often publish readers' tips and suggestions for simplifying and improving family living.

You will need to decide what types of letters will be published in your magazine. A magazine about movies might publish reader's letters that critique current movies, while a fashion magazine might include letters that offer makeup and fashion tips. Decide on a title for your Mailbox page that is appropriate for the type of letters you will include. Refer to the worksheet and writing steps on page 22, and review the Mailbox page samples on page 23 to help you get started.

Getting Down to the Business of Writing   Name _____

The Mailbox Page Worksheet

1. What type of letters will your magazine publish (tips from readers, editorial comments about previous articles, etc.)?
   _____

2. What will be the title of your Mailbox page? _____

3. List six possible topics for letters that would be appropriate for your group's magazine.
   _____
   _____
   _____
   _____

4. Who will write your group's Mailbox page? _____

Steps for Writing the Mailbox Page

1. Using the information you recorded above and referring to the two Mailbox page samples on page 23, write a first draft of five to ten potential letters for your own Mailbox page.
2. Enlist the help of other group members in revising your letters and choosing the best three to six to be included on your final Mailbox page.
3. Arrange your selected revised letters in an interesting way on a page headed with the title you selected for your Mailbox page. Reread the layout tips listed on page 14.
4. Store your completed Mailbox page in your group's "Completed Works" folder.

Create a Magazine
© The Learning Works, Inc.

Reader's Ramblings

(sample letters from a magazine covering the subject of television programming)

I enjoyed last week's issue highlighting sitcoms of the 1960s. The article, "Remember When . . ." made me laugh and cry at once at the memories of yesteryears on the tube. Thanks for your fine coverage of the Golden Years of television!

—R. Reynolds
Palo Alto, CA

John Gross's article in the May issue of *TV TIMES* singing the praises of filmmakers who bring old television show characters back to life in new movies neglected to point out the negative aspects of the practice. First of all, television programs are intended to be an hour long at the most and seldom make interesting two-hour shows. Secondly, the programs selected to be turned into movies are seldom of high quality, often outdated, and nearly always targeted at the lowest denominator of our fine population.

—P. Rodriguez
Albany, NY

Reader Tips

(sample letters from a parenting magazine)

The bedtime routine of brushing teeth, changing into pajamas, and reading stories used to drag on forever with my children, but I found that by starting the routine 30 minutes earlier and treating the kids to extra story time when they complete their bedtime preparations early, I've made my little ones quite speedy at getting ready for bed.

—C. Taylor
Minneapolis, MN

Enlisting the help of children in household chores during the summer months when sunshine, neighborhood kids, and baseball games all beckon can be a real challenge. I've got some great helpers at my house, though. We recently enacted a rule that says all of the day's chores must be completed *before* anyone walks out the door to join in a soccer game, swim in a pool, or ride bikes with friends!

—R. Steinberg
Waltham, MA

Special Report

Occasionally something so newsworthy happens that a magazine's editors decide to devote additional space to the event or topic. The extra coverage may come in the form of a special report. A special report might include a cover article, several related articles, photographs, timelines, charts, graphs, and other documents that address a topic in-depth. A science magazine might include a special report on an ongoing situation such as global warming, while a music magazine might dedicate additional space to the death of a superstar.

Your group will decide on an event or topic that might warrant a special report in your magazine, what approaches will be used to cover the news, and which group members will be responsible for the completion of your special report. Use the worksheet, writing steps, and samples on pages 25–26 to assist your group in completing this project.

Getting Down to the Business of Writing   Name _____

Special Report Worksheet

1. Brainstorm several topics for special reports that would fit the theme of your magazine and list them here.

   _____

   _____

2. Choose one of the topics listed above and record it here.

   _____

3. Decide on three or four formats your group will use to cover the topic selected (cover story, charts, timelines, interviews, graphs, etc.) and list them here.

   _____

   _____

4. What specific aspect of your Special Report topic will be covered by each item?

   _____

   _____

   _____

   _____

5. Select titles for your Special Report and its individual parts and list them here.

   _____

   _____

6. Which group member(s) will work on your magazine's Special Report articles?

   _____

   _____

Steps for Writing a Special Report

1. Write a Special Report cover article introducing readers to the Special Report theme. Tell what articles, interviews, charts, etc., will address the theme.
2. Write a first draft of each Special Report item.
3. Enlist the help of your group members in revising your Special Report items for content and mechanical improvements.
4. Create professional-looking final drafts of your Special Report documents and store them in your group's "Completed Works" folder.

On Beyond Basics

(a Special Report cover story sample)

New information in the fields of science, technology, and medicine is emerging faster than most of us can keep up with. So how are we to prepare our youth for the 21st century? Experts answer this question in varying ways. While some insist on teaching a core battery of facts and skills, others suggest kids need to be taught how to locate information and make use of computers and calculators rather than wasting time on memorizing times tables they will never use and learning scientific theories that will be outdated before they graduate. Some experts demand that schools teach self-esteem, problem-solving skills, conflict management, and moral reasoning to students who are not being "socialized" by working parents who no longer spend enough hours at home in a week to teach such basics.

New educational approaches are popping up everywhere in response to these and other modern educational theories. There is no longer a single approach to teaching our youth. Charter schools, alternative schools, home schooling, public schools, and private schools are just some of the choices parents are confronted with in deciding how best to prepare their children for adulthood.

In this issue of *Education Today*, a Special Report on "Educating Students for the 21st Century" includes a question-and-answer article on types of schools; an exclusive interview with Professor of Technology in Education, Jerry Thomas; a pictorial of successful schools entitled "Pictures of Success," and a variety of charts, graphs, and facts about what you can expect from the world of education today and tomorrow.

Little Brick Schoolhouse

(a Special Report chart sample)

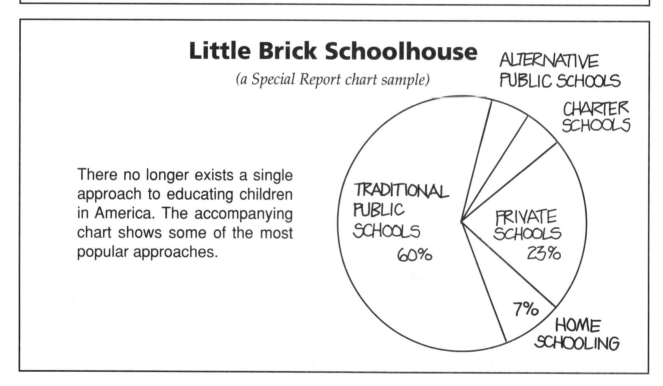

There no longer exists a single approach to educating children in America. The accompanying chart shows some of the most popular approaches.

Profiles and Interviews

No matter what its subject matter, a magazine usually provides information about influential people whose works or lives are in some way related to the magazine's theme. *Profiles* are third-person accounts that provide personal and/or professional biographical information about an intriguing person, or tell a theme-related story about a specific incident in a featured person's life. Interviews provide a forum for direct quotes. *Interviews* often are written in a question-and-answer format.

Several factors are considered in deciding whether to include a profile or an interview in a magazine. Profiles work best when an author wishes to discuss a featured person's life or career. Interviews are most often used for promotional purposes such as selling a new book or movie, or when some controversy is involved, because the featured person can be asked direct questions. Inspirational stories about heroic accomplishments are best presented as profiles since the third-person writing style avoids the appearance of bragging.

Decide with your group whether your magazine will include an interview or a profile. Then refer to the questions, steps, and sample that follow to help you get started. In most cases, the profile or interview you write for your magazine will be a "mock" document in which you make up the questions, answers, and/or biographical details of your featured person's life or story since you are not likely to find a "real" specialist or personality in your magazine's field to interview directly.

Getting Down to the Business of Writing   Name _____

Profile and Interview Worksheet

1. Which group member(s) will be responsible for writing the profile or interview?
   _____

2. What fictitious, or actual, person will you be writing about for your magazine? (Be sure your person is related in some way to your magazine's theme.)
   _____

3. Will you conduct an interview or write a profile? Explain your choice.
   _____
   _____

4. What details, story, or subjects will your profile or interview include?
   _____
   _____
   _____

Steps for Writing a Profile or Interview

1. Referring to your answers above and the sample profile on page 29, write the first draft of your magazine's profile or interview.
2. Revise your first draft with the help of other group members.
3. Type a professional-looking final draft of your profile or interview. If you use a question-and-answer format, experiment with different type fonts, sizes, and styles (e.g., bold and italics) to introduce new questions and answers.
4. Add an appropriate title to your profile or interview.
5. Place your completed interview or profile in your group's "Completed Works" folder.

Mom Scores Big Points at Home and on the Court

(a sample profile of a fictitious character)

Sheila Carter plays basketball for the newly-formed NWBA. She also cleans house, drives a carpool to preschool, and shares meal preparation and dishwashing duties with her husband, Jason. Sheila, mother of four-year-old Taylor and two-year-old Jordan, is happy to oblige. Both motherhood and basketball stardom have been her dreams since childhood.

Sheila began watching her older brother, James, play basketball when she was just two weeks old. That's when Sheila and her parents saw James receive the Most Valuable Player Award at the 1977 Colorado State High School Basketball Championship games. Although highly successful in both high school and college basketball, James' greatest basketball accomplishment may have been encouraging his sister's outstanding natural talent. Today, it is Sheila who is winning awards.

Sheila gives James much of the credit for her skills in dribbling, shooting, and passing. James supervised her in endless hours of drills and practice from the time she was a young girl. The determination paid off. Sheila now plays professional ball *and* parents two children whom she encourages in talents of their own—finger-painting and nursery rhyme recitation!

Poetry and Short Stories

Your magazine will showcase not only your group's journalistic skills but also its creative writing abilities. One to three pages of your magazine will be dedicated to theme-related poetry or short stories. Poems may take any form—from free verse to cinquains, from sonnets to haikus. One long poem may fill the entire space designated for poetry or several shorter ones may be arranged on the page. One author may write all of the poems you include, or several group members may each contribute a poem or two to the poetry pages. Group members may also work in teams to create poems.

Instead of poetry pages, your group may elect to include a short story in your magazine. If so, be sure it contains all of the elements of an effective story including a well-developed plot and story line with a clear beginning, middle, and end; a definite and descriptive setting; well-defined characters who experience growth; and a conflict that gets resolved by the story's end.

Refer to the worksheet, writing steps, and samples on the following pages to help you create your short story or poetry pages.

Getting Down to the Business of Writing   Name _____

Poetry and Short Stories Worksheet

1. Will your magazine contain a single long poem, several shorter poems, or a short story?
   _____

2. Who will write your poetry or short story page(s)? If your magazine will include several poems, will they all be written by a single group member or by several group members?
   _____
   _____

3. What will be the theme of your poems or the plot of your story? How does this theme or plot relate to the overall theme of your magazine?
   _____
   _____
   _____

4. If you will be writing poems, what forms will they take? If you will be writing a short story, what conflict will be resolved by the end? Who are the main characters of the story?
   _____
   _____
   _____
   _____

Steps for Writing Poetry and Short Stories

1. Write a first draft of your poem(s) or short story.
2. Allow fellow group members to suggest changes in both content and mechanics that will improve your draft.
3. Develop a title and an interesting layout for your page. Maintain plenty of white space and consider including pictures or drawings.
4. Place your completed short story or poetry page in your group's "Completed Works" folder.

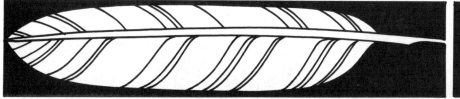

In Other Words . . .
(poetry page samples)

Basketball

Basketball
Fast, loud, fun
Dribbling, passing, shooting
Making the shot
Awesome sport

Summer Vacation

Important dates in history
Geometric formulas
Reading, writing, drawing
Singing and playing the clarinet
State capitals and famous rivers
The Constitution and amendments
My brain is full and might explode
If tomorrow weren't
The last day of school

New Products Preview

Whatever the theme of your group's magazine, it will include a page dedicated to evaluating real or imagined new products that might interest the reader. A music magazine might preview soon-to-be-released compact discs or new sound system equipment. A pet magazine might feature a story on a new grooming product or highlight the benefits of a new dog food formula. Regardless of the specific items previewed, the completion of the New Products Preview page will give you a chance to try your hand at *evaluative writing*.

Writing evaluations requires that you accurately describe your product, critically consider its pros and cons, compare and contrast it with similar products, and draw logical conclusions about the product's overall value. Use the worksheet, writing steps, and sample Preview page that follow to help you develop an effective New Products Preview page.

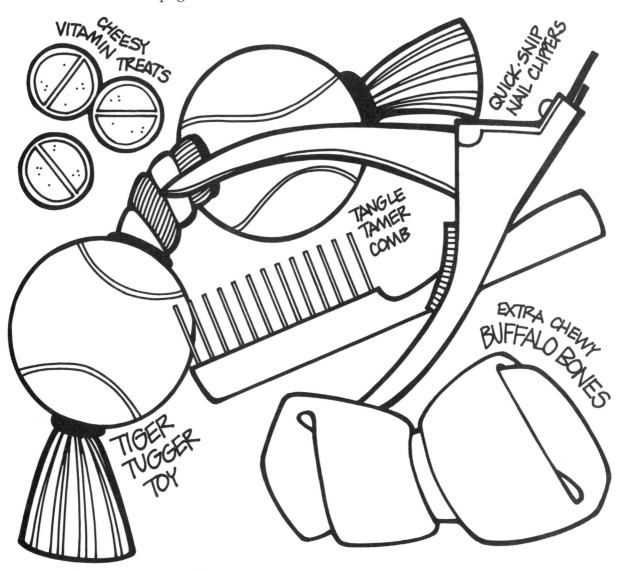

Getting Down to the Business of Writing   Name _____

New Products Preview Worksheet

1. You may choose to write an in-depth review of a single new product, or you may write shorter reviews of several products. List the one to six theme-related products you will preview in your magazine.

   _____
   _____

2. Describe the products you will be evaluating.

   _____
   _____
   _____

3. List the strengths and weaknesses of each product.

   _____
   _____
   _____

4. How do the products you will be reviewing compare to similar products? How do they differ? How would you rate each product overall?

   _____
   _____
   _____
   _____
   _____

Steps for Writing a New Products Preview Page

1. Decide whether you will thoroughly review a single product or more broadly summarize several products.
2. In turn, describe the products you will preview. Compare and contrast them with similar products. Describe their benefits and drawbacks, and give an overall opinion.
3. Enlist the help of other group members in revising your first draft.
4. Add a theme-related title, and arrange the product previews in an interesting layout. Add pictures and/or drawings. For your subheadings, experiment with different type styles and sizes.
5. Store the completed New Products Preview page in your group's "Completed Works" folder.

Create a Magazine
© The Learning Works, Inc.

Bon Appetit

(a New Products Preview page sample)

Grandma Bonnie's Creative Cookies Company, Inc., introduces a new line of cookies this month, marketed to adults and kids alike. The kickoff of "Crummy Cookies" will be accompanied by some pretty funny television advertisements which will begin airing Tuesday, April 13. In one ad, a young woman at a party attempts to restrain herself from sampling Grandma Bonnie's Crummy Cookies as she watches all the other party guests eating them with gusto. A grandmotherly woman notices the longing on the woman's face and offers her one of the cookies, saying, "Try one, dear. Crumbs don't have calories," at which point the woman smiles and tries two or three. A voice-over announces, "Grandma Bonnie's new Crummy Cookies may not be calorie-free, but like all of Grandma Bonnie's goodies, they are all-natural; contain no fat, sugar, or oil; and are 100% irresistible."

Cute commercials may help to sell a product, but they can't make a product taste good. But, in this case, they don't need to! Crummy Cookies come in six flavors—and they're all delicious! The chocolate chip variety is one of the best brands of chocolate chip cookies available on the market. In a recent taste-test, consumers even preferred Crummy Cookies to those oven-fresh, 350-calorie cookies you can buy at the mall—and Crummy Cookies are much less expensive.

Just as the commercial says, all of Grandma Bonnie's baked goods are fat-free and sugar-free, low in calories, and contain no preservatives. They are highly recommended for anyone with a sweet tooth!

"A Look Back" or "Future Forward"

The theme of your group's magazine may have a history, and you can add interest to your magazine by including a column exploring that history. Check news magazines or other periodicals to see how a history page can be set up. Sometimes a chart will compare historical news with news from the present. Sometimes an in-depth article will summarize an interesting story from history.

The theme of your magazine may work better with a forward-looking comparison. If your magazine covers the sport of snowboarding, for example, you might want to compare and contrast aspects of this relatively new sport with "snowboarding of the future." You could discuss such topics as equipment advances and increases in participation.

You may choose to write in paragraph form for this project, or you may take a timeline or chart approach. The worksheet, writing steps, and sample which follow will help you get started.

Getting Down to the Business of Writing Name _____

"A Look Back" or "Future Forward" Worksheet

1. What real or imagined theme-related events will your column cover?
   _____
   _____

2. What details will make these events interesting to your readers? How might these details relate to the lives of today's readers?
   _____
   _____
   _____

3. Will you create a chart, a timeline, or a full-length article to convey the information you wish to cover?
   _____

4. Which group member(s) will write your column?
   _____

5. What will be the title of your page?
   _____

Writing Steps

1. If you are writing a full-length story about a real or imagined theme-related event, write the first draft as a short story or a news report with a clear beginning, middle, and end. If you are creating a chart, graph, or timeline, include enough text to make the chart easy to read and meaningful to the reader.
2. Present your first draft to group members, and ask them to help you decide if you have used the most effective approach in conveying your information. Also enlist their help in proofreading and making revisions.
3. Create a professional-looking final draft of your document and store it in your group's "Completed Works" folder.

Create a Magazine
© The Learning Works, Inc.

This Week in Movie History

(a sample column)

As we kick off this summer's cinematic season with horror and humor, romance and drama, let's stop to reflect on some of the movies of past summer seasons that coaxed viewers off the hot streets and into air-conditioned theaters.

Benji, 1973

What would summer be without movies for the kids? In 1973, a tale of a heroic dog who saves some adorable young people from some less-than-adorable kidnappers won the hearts of America's youth and their parents. Still available on video, Benji was an instant box office hit more than 25 years ago.

Invasion of the Body Snatchers, 1956

Remade several times, the original version of Jack Finney's famous science fiction story starring Kevin McCarthy startled many folks in the summer of 1956, and continues to be a video store sell-out today. The 1978 version with Donald Sutherland and Jeff Goldblum is worth a look, too.

The Three Stooges Meet Hercules, 1962

Time travel, Siamese-twin Cyclops, Hercules, and the slapstick humor of the ever-lovable Three Stooges made this flick so popular that the fun and fumbling fools got together two more times over the course of a year to offer moviegoers *The Three Stooges in Orbit* (1962) and *The Three Stooges Go Around the World in a Daze* (1963).

How-To's: Writing Instructions

Some magazines include articles that instruct readers on how to create a craft project, apply makeup, make simple repairs, or improve an interpersonal relationship. While the topics addressed in how-to and self-help articles vary according to the theme of the magazine, most of these articles follow a format that provides clear and concise instructions. Often the instructions are presented as a list of steps or key points followed by a discussion of each.

With your other group members, decide on a theme-appropriate topic for your how-to page. Depending on your magazine's overall theme, you may choose to write instructions for the creation of something tangible or give advice on how to change a behavior, improve a skill, or learn something new. Simplify the instructions you write for your how-to page by adding photographs, drawings, diagrams, or charts. (Be sure to give credit for any photographs or drawings obtained from another publication.) You may also want to break your suggestions into numbered steps or short phrases introduced by subtitles. The worksheet, writing steps, and sample that follow will help you get started.

Getting Down to the Business of Writing

Name _____

How-To Worksheet

1. What topic will your instructional article cover?
   _____

2. Will you need to complete research to instruct others on your topic? If so, where will you find your information?
   _____

3. Will you organize your instructions as numbered steps, short phrases introduced by subheadings, or some other format (specify)?
   _____

4. Will you add drawings or photographs to your instructional article? Where will you get the photographs or who will draw the pictures?
   _____

5. What will you title your How-To page?
   _____

6. Who will write your How-To page?
   _____

Steps for Writing a How-To Page

1. Conduct any research necessary for the completion of your How-To page.
2. Write an introductory paragraph summarizing what you will be teaching.
3. Divide your topic into short steps, and write a sentence or two describing each step in order.
4. Create a first draft of your How-To page by organizing your information into numbered steps or subdivisions with headings.
5. Allow other group members to read your instructions for clarity and to make suggestions for revisions. Also allow them to proofread your article for mechanical errors.
6. Add appropriate pictures, drawings, graphs, etc., to your final draft. Store your completed How-To article in your group's "Completed Works" folder.

Flying Colors: How to Pass Any Test, Anytime

(a sample How-To page)

Earning good grades requires more than listening to teachers and completing homework assignments. You've got to do well on tests. So read on and learn how to pass any test with flying colors.

Short Answer and Essay Tests

In an attempt to encourage critical thinking skills, teachers today employ short answer and essay tests more often than any other testing style. Even a math teacher might ask students to write a short paragraph explaining how they arrived at their answers. To do well on short answer and essay tests, you need to:

1. Understand the question. *Compare, contrast, explain, examine, define, describe,* and other essay test verbs all have distinct meanings. Be sure you know exactly what the question is before you attempt to answer it.

2. Write in complete sentences. Unless you are asked specifically for a chart, graph, or diagram, answer short answer and essay questions in complete and organized sentences or paragraphs.

3. Stick to the point. A long, rambling answer will *not* impress your teacher. You should be able to answer a short answer question in one to two sentences and an essay question in one to two paragraphs. Be concise—and stick to the question being asked.

True-False and Multiple Choice Tests

Do your best on questions that provide you with a choice by:

1. Quickly answering all questions you are sure about. As you work, be certain to fill in the blank or bubble that corresponds to each question.

2. Identifying incorrect answers on questions you are not as sure about.

3. Making educated guesses using the remaining answer choices by applying what knowledge you do have about the subject area being tested.

Fill-in-the-Blank Tests

This type of test requires that you know your stuff—especially if answer choices are not provided. Follow these steps in answering fill-in-the-blank tests:

1. First answer all questions you are certain about.

2. Make educated guesses about remaining questions, being sure the word you fill in the blank makes sense when read as part of the entire test sentence or question.

Remember: Whatever the test type, *be prepared.* Study, bring extra pens and pencils, be rested, and do your best. Good luck!

Voice of the Critic: Recommending Events and Activities

Just as the completion of the New Products Preview page allowed you to practice critical evaluation skills, writing a review of events and activities related to your magazine's theme will hone your ability to voice your opinion intelligently. It is not enough for the critic of a play to say that he or she did not like the performance, the critic must give sound reasons for his or her opinion.

You will create a Voice of the Critic page for your magazine in which you write intelligently about a real or fictitious play, museum or aquarium exhibit, concert, movie, or other theme-related event(s). Before you begin, look at the sample review on page 44. Then use the worksheet and writing steps on page 43 to help you in writing your own Voice of the Critic page.

Getting Down to the Business of Writing   Name _____

Voice of the Critic Worksheet

1. What real or fictitious events or activities related to your magazine's theme will you review? Will you write an in-depth review of a single activity, or several shorter commentaries?

2. Describe each event you will review. _____
   _____
   _____
   _____

3. What did you like about the event(s) being reviewed? _____
   _____
   _____

4. What did you dislike about the event(s) being reviewed? _____
   _____
   _____

5. What was your overall opinion of the event(s) being reviewed? _____
   _____
   _____

6. Which group member(s) will write your review? _____
   _____

7. What will you call your Voice of the Critic page? _____
   _____

Steps for Writing the Voice of the Critic Page

1. Describe each event you are reviewing, perhaps comparing it to similar events and highlighting the unique aspects of the reviewed event.
2. Tell about the positive and negative aspects of the event(s) being reviewed.
3. Give your overall opinion of the event(s). Would you recommend the event(s) to readers? Why or why not?
4. Ask group members to help you revise the first draft of your page.
5. Create a professional-looking final copy of your Voice of the Critic page. Consider adding photographs, drawings, or another design element. Store your final copy in your group's "Completed Works" folder.

Create a Magazine
© The Learning Works, Inc.

San Francisco Sights

—by Mai Matsura

(a Voice of the Critic page sample)

Golden Gate Park

Museums, an aquarium, hiking and biking trails, and a beautiful 50-acre arboretum grace this popular park at the foot of the Golden Gate Bridge. Visitors can enjoy a stroll, a barbecue, a football game, or some good old-fashioned people watching in this scenic location that spells San Francisco.

The Sea Cliff District

Elaborate mansions lining the bay create a scenic display for sightseers who drive through the Sea Cliff District; but for those tourists interested in getting out of the car or off the tour bus, this residential area has little to offer.

Fisherman's Wharf

Fresh clam chowder served in an edible sourdough bread bowl makes the Wharf a favorite among locals and tourists alike. If you are on a family trip, tour the wax museum or Ripley's Believe It or Not. Save up for this stop though; it's a bit pricey.

The Exploratorium

The young and the young-at-heart will enjoy this hands-on science museum that offers constant favorites like the Shadow Box, and periodically-changing exhibits that explore anything from brains to robots to natural disasters. If you are a tourist, schedule at least five hours for this stop. If you live in the Bay Area, ask your child's teacher to look into the Exploratorium Classroom projects offered all year long.

Pier 39

Specialty stores and restaurants offer patrons of Pier 39 everything from music boxes to cotton candy. Some people would say that you haven't seen the City by the Bay until you've been to the pier, but San Francisco has a lot more to offer than this showy tourist trap.

Chinatown

Be sure to take the cable car to Chinatown before leaving San Francisco. You'll find remarkable bargains, incredible Chinese food; and a variety of imports—from cool slippers to chess sets to jewelry. Chinatown offers unbeatable fun!

Getting Down to the Business of Writing

Advice Column: Writing Questions and Answers

Newspapers and magazines often carry a column that answers theme-related questions from readers. A medical doctor will answer medical questions, an expert on etiquette will answer questions pertaining to manners and social situations, and a therapist will answer questions concerning family issues, interpersonal relations, or psychological health.

You and the other members of your group are experts on the concerns of young people. As such, together you will create an Advice Column for your magazine. If your magazine's audience is teenagers, you do not need to stick to the theme of your magazine for this activity, but may address any issues that pertain to your magazine's young audience. If your magazine is targeted to a different or more generalized population (children, senior citizens, athletes, etc.), you may choose to address either the general concerns of your target audience or create a column that addresses questions pertaining only to your magazine's specific theme.

Answer the worksheet questions on the next page, read the Advice Column sample letters, and follow the writing steps provided as your group works cooperatively to create your magazine's Advice Column page.

Advice Column Worksheet

1. Will your Advice Column address the general concerns of teenagers, the general concerns of an alternative target audience, or questions pertaining to your magazine's specific theme?
   _____

2. Your column will include at least one question/answer pair from each of your group members. How many question-answer pairs will your column include altogether?
   _____

3. Who will lay out your Advice Column and type the final draft?
   _____

Steps for Writing the Advice Column Page

1. As a group, choose one member to coordinate this activity and keep all of the group's members on track.
2. Have each student in your group write one or two questions for your page.
3. Exchange papers and allow each student to answer a question that he or she did not write.
4. Exchange papers again and have each group member read aloud a question/answer pair that he or she did not work on.
5. Consider each question/answer pair in turn. As a group, suggest improvements, make revisions, and keep or eliminate question-answer pairs as the group sees fit. (Remember that the final draft will include at least one question from each group member.) Add new question/answer pairs if necessary, and make suggestions for the title and layout of the final draft of your Advice Column page.
6. Select a group member to type the final draft of your Advice Column. Place the completed page in your group's "Completed Works" folder.

Advice Column

(sample letters)

Dear Jim,

My little brother is a pest! He breaks my things, he tries to start fake sword fights by stabbing me with a broomstick, and he follows my friends around—that is, when I can convince them to come over at all! My mom does nothing to help. She thinks kids should work out their own problems. What do you think?

—signed, Fed Up in Florida

Dear Fed Up,

Unless your brother's antics create a dangerous situation, I think your mom is probably right. Working out your problems with your brother is a great way to learn how to get along with the "pests" that will present themselves throughout your life. In the case of your little brother, it sounds like he likes you a lot—maybe even idolizes you a bit—and really wants your attention. Try offering it to him in a positive way by taking him to the park or reading him stories, and see if the negative behaviors stop. Good luck!

Dear Christine,

End a long-running debate between my mom and me. Do you think a seventh grader ought to be able to wear makeup to school?

—signed, Wondering

Dear Wondering,

There are no one-size-fits-all rules about the age at which kids ought to be able to try new things. Your opinions and your mother's must both be taken into consideration in the decision about when you can wear makeup to school. Before you talk to your mom about it again, consider your reasons for wanting to wear makeup. If you are trying to fit in with your friends or create self-confidence by hiding behind a mask, your mom may be right in thinking your reasons are not sound. On the other hand, if you want to use light makeup to accentuate beauty or to cover the blemishes that sometimes appear during the teenage years, your mom may be more inclined to see your views. Just remember to speak calmly to your mother. Save the big battles for the big issues.

Getting Down to the Business of Writing

What's New? Reporting on the News, Sports, and Entertainment

Your group's magazine will include a page of journalistic reporting on some topic that will fit the theme of your magazine. An entertainment magazine will report on some news from the entertainment world and a sports magazine usually will cover one or two major sporting events.

Keep in mind that news stories are concisely-worded articles that inform the reader of who, what, where, when, why, and how something happened. News stories should be written from an *objective* point of view. If you are ecstatic that your team won the pennant, this is not the place to voice your excitement. Save emotions and subjective opinions for your magazine's essay page. Just stick to the facts on the news page.

Complete the worksheet on the following page before you try your hand at writing a news article. Then use the writing steps and sample provided to guide you in reporting your story.

Getting Down to the Business of Writing   Name _____

"What's New?" Worksheet

1. What theme-related story will you write about? In a short phrase tell about the

   Who: _____

   What: _____
   _____

   Where: _____

   When: _____

   Why: _____
   _____

   How: _____

2. Think of a catchy, concise title for your news story, and record it here.

   _____

Steps for Writing the "What's New?" Story

1. Practice locating the *who, what, where, when, why,* and *how* in the sample news story on the next page and in several articles from your local newspaper.
2. Write a first draft of your own story. Remember to word your story concisely, speak from an objective point of view, and include the who, what, where, when, why, and how of the story.
3. Allow group members to help you revise your first draft with a focus on clarity and mechanics.
4. Write the final draft of your news story in a two-column format. Maintain plenty of white space, and add a photograph or drawing if space permits.

Local Kids Save Senior Citizens' Morning Meals Program

(a sample news story)

Senior citizens hold a special place in the heart of Anne Baker, a middle school history teacher. As a college student, she worked in nursing homes. Currently, she makes weekly visits to elderly shut-ins in her community—and her commitment to caring for the elderly continues to strengthen. Last September, Mrs. Baker introduced her 13- and 14-year-old history students from Marks Middle School to a whole new world when she set up the Cross-Generation Information Exchange Program (CIEP). The CIEP is a program in which residents from the Chatham Senior Living Apartments teach hobbies such as woodcarving and knitting to Mrs. Baker's students, and Mrs. Baker's students teach Chatham residents how to use computer graphics programs and music synthesizers.

These teaching opportunities occur monthly when seniors and students take turns visiting each other. In addition to sharing skills and hobbies, CIEP participants entertain each other with concerts, skits, stories, and speeches—and share great food at pizza parties, English teas, and ice cream socials.

It was during one of those ice cream socials that Chatham resident Ada Jones told Marks student Jackie Seaton that the city's Morning Meals Program, which offers free breakfasts to low-income senior residents, was going to cease operations due to budget cuts. When outraged Marks students took over the program themselves, cooking daily meals before school and raising funds and shopping for groceries after school, the city was so impressed with the demonstration of care and effort that they put the program back into the budget. Now the city raises the funds, does the shopping, and cooks the Morning Meals again, but Marks students continue to share skills, food, and fun with their friends at Chatham.

Essays and Opinions

Magazine editors often place an essay or opinion piece on one of the first or last pages of their publication. Opinion pieces may also appear as part of a Special Report. Always labeled as such, essays are not intended to be informative so much as thought-provoking. They assume the reader has acquired basic details on their topic of discussion by reading columns elsewhere in the magazine. Therefore, an essay often focuses on a single aspect of a large story, offers suggested reasons behind a story or possible solutions to problems mentioned in a story, demonstrates a connection between seemingly unrelated aspects of a story, or looks at a story from an unpopular, unique, or unexpected perspective.

Essay and opinion pieces always declare strong points. Often they use humor, satire, anecdotes, emotional appeals, and/or facts and statistics to do so. A magazine issue that includes a Special Report on crime might feature an essay that discusses possible causes of crime, or an opinion piece that focuses on a single aspect of the problem, such as teenage crime, urban crime, white-collar crime, or press coverage of crime.

As you prepare to write an essay for your magazine, be sure to choose a topic that is covered by at least one story elsewhere in your magazine, and have firmly in mind the point you will be making *before* you begin writing. Use the worksheet, writing steps, and sample that follow to help you get started.

Getting Down to the Business of Writing   Name _____

Essays and Opinions Worksheet

1. Choose a topic (covered in at least one other article in your magazine) for your essay or opinion piece, and record it here.
   _____

2. Describe the specific aspect of the topic your essay will cover (e.g., causes of a situation, potential solutions, personal experience, unique perspective, etc.).
   _____

3. In one sentence, write the point your essay will make.
   _____

4. In order to make your argument convincing, you will have to anticipate objections or see the other side of the issue. List viewpoints that differ from the point you will make and explain how you might answer each objection.
   _____
   _____
   _____

5. What writing style will you use to make your point? Choose one or more of the following approaches: humor, satire, first-person narrative, persuasive essay, emotional appeals, anecdotes, statistics and facts.
   _____

6. What will you title your essay?
   _____

Steps for Writing Essay and Opinion Pieces

1. Introduce your topic or subtopic with a startling statistic, thoughtful quote, intriguing anecdote, or another attention-grabbing device.
2. Build up to your point in the body of your essay by including facts, statistics, personal experiences, counters to anticipated objections, and other approaches you selected for #5, above.
3. Conclude your essay with a strong statement. Use the sentence you wrote for #3, or reword that sentence to make the same point.
4. Allow fellow group members to assist you in revising your essay for clarity and mechanical accuracy.
5. Type a professional-looking final draft of your essay, and store it in your group's "Completed Works" file.

Create a Magazine
© The Learning Works, Inc.

Too Much of a Good Thing

(a sample essay)

startling statistic

Within a 25-mile radius of my home, I can shop at any one of four fully-enclosed malls, six extensive strip malls, or countless shopping centers. I can spend my money at shoe stores, toy stores, bookstores, grocery stores, computer stores, clothing stores, kitchenware stores, department stores, or novelty shops. At my neighborhood shoe store, I can purchase work shoes, dress shoes, jogging shoes, basketball shoes, cowboy boots, or sandals. If I really love sandals, I can walk out the door of that one store with 26 pair—all in my size—but different in style, color, or design.

anticipated objection

My situation is not unique because I live in the suburbs. My urban friends may find themselves in corner shops instead of strip malls, and my rural companions may drive a few extra miles to their consumer outlets, but we all have more material choices than we know what to do with! So what? America was built on the concept of free choice. Capitalism and free enterprise drive our economy. The more the better. Right?

facts

At the turn of the century no one owned more than a single pair of work shoes. Houses were built with only one closet to accommodate the wardrobes of an entire six member family. During the Great Depression children played with dolls made of potatoes. Bread and soup might be a family's only meal choice for a month. Today, choices in food and dolls and everything else are staggering. Certainly we've greatly improved our standard of living.

emotional appeal

But at what price? America's landfills overflow as we drink juice out of single-serving containers, and replace mechanically sound automobiles with newer models every two or three years. Rain forests diminish and the ozone layer becomes depleted to appease our unquenchable thirst for more and faster and better.

the point

Having the freedom to choose between twenty-six different styles whenever we want to buy new sandals is not worth the destruction of our planet. Let's start using our free choice to choose consumer moderation and global restoration.

Getting Down to the Business of Writing   Name _____

Keeping Track

Record your group's progress on your magazine's core articles here.

Article Name	Author	First Draft Due Date	Final Draft Due Date
(A Word from the Editor)			
(Contributors' Corner)			
(The Mailbox)			
(Special Report Cover Article)			
(Special Report Article)			
(Special Report Article)			
(Profile or Interview)			
(Short Story or Poetry Page)			
(New Products Preview)			
("A Look Back" or "Future Forward")			
(How-To Page)			
(Voice of the Critic)			
(Advice Column)			
(What's New?)			
(Essay Page)			

Create a Magazine
© The Learning Works, Inc.

Section III
Creating Your Magazine

ARTICLES

fashion pages

FRONT COVER **back cover**

Creating Your Magazine   Name _____

Designing the Front Cover

Your magazine's cover should reflect the general theme and specific articles of your project. It should include a picture, a title, and a number of article titles and short phrase article descriptions. You will also need to include the issue date and the price. Your cover picture should feature a drawing by the most artistic member of your group. If no one in your group is artistically inclined, locate some appropriate clip art from a computer program or a picture from a book or magazine that could be traced or copied. (Be sure to give credit for any artwork obtained from another source.)

Brainstorm ideas for your magazine's cover, and use the lines below to record your group's responses.

Possible picture ideas that would illustrate your magazine's overall theme or the theme of a specific feature article:

_____
_____
_____

Ideas for article titles and short, catchy phrases that will motivate readers to buy your magazine:

_____
_____
_____

On a separate piece of paper, sketch some possible arrangements for your magazine's front cover elements (graphics and words). With the other members of your group, choose one idea and create a front cover for your magazine.

Creating Your Magazine   Name _____

Adding the Ads

What would a magazine be without advertisements? It probably wouldn't exist. Advertisements help pay for a magazine's publication. Marketing teams work to ensure that the advertisements that fill the pages of their periodicals will appeal to the magazine's target audience. A great deal of marketing research goes into determining what types of ads will interest a magazine's readers.

Working as a group, answer the questions and follow the steps below to help you create effective ads for your publication.

Answer the following questions about your magazine's targeted audience.

1. List five or more products they are likely to purchase often.

   _____
   _____
   _____

2. Will they appreciate ads with strong visual effects, clever words, and/or matter-of-fact information about products?

   _____

3. Will they prefer serious ads or funny ones? _____

Follow the steps below to create at least four advertisements for your magazine:

1. As a group, decide on the products you will advertise.
2. Work in pairs to create ads for your selected products. Remember that ads should include both words and pictures. Short, catchy phrases are usually more effective in advertisements than long, complex sentences.
3. Play with the layout of your ads until you come up with effective presentations. (See the sample ads on page 58.)
4. Have each pair of students share its ad with the rest of the group, and take suggestions for revisions.
5. Each pair of students should create a final draft of their ad to be placed in your group's "Completed Works" folder. All of theses ads will appear in your final magazine.

Sample Advertisements

Creating Your Magazine   Name _____

It's the "In" Thing: Adding Fashion Pages

Some topics lend themselves to pictures more readily than to words. Fashion magazines are filled with glossy pictures of hair styles, clothing styles, and accessories; car magazines display automobiles; and magazines dedicated to interior decorating include pictures of living rooms and bathrooms and closets.

Whether the theme of your magazine is beauty or bicycles, you will create at least one page dedicated to a pictorial display of "fashion"—anything that is in style in the field your magazine covers. Answer the questions below and check out the sample on page 60 to help you get started.

1. Who will produce your fashion page? _____

2. What will be the theme of your fashion page (cars, clothes, CDs, etc.)?
   _____

3. Will your fashion page include drawings, clip art, photographs, pictures cut out of real magazines or some other display? (Remember to give credit if you use someone else's work.)
   _____

4. What will be the title of your fashion page?
   _____

5. Write a caption for each picture you include on your fashion page. On a separate piece of paper, sketch possible arrangements of your pictures and captions. Present your fashion page to your group members for revision. Work with the other members of your group to create a final draft. Place your finished page in your group's "Completed Works" folder.

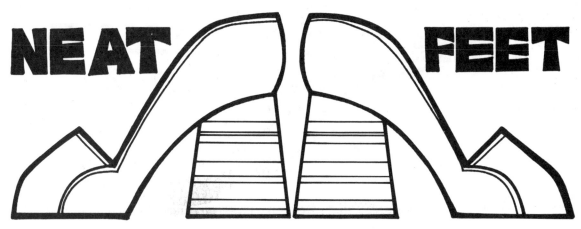

Creating Your Magazine

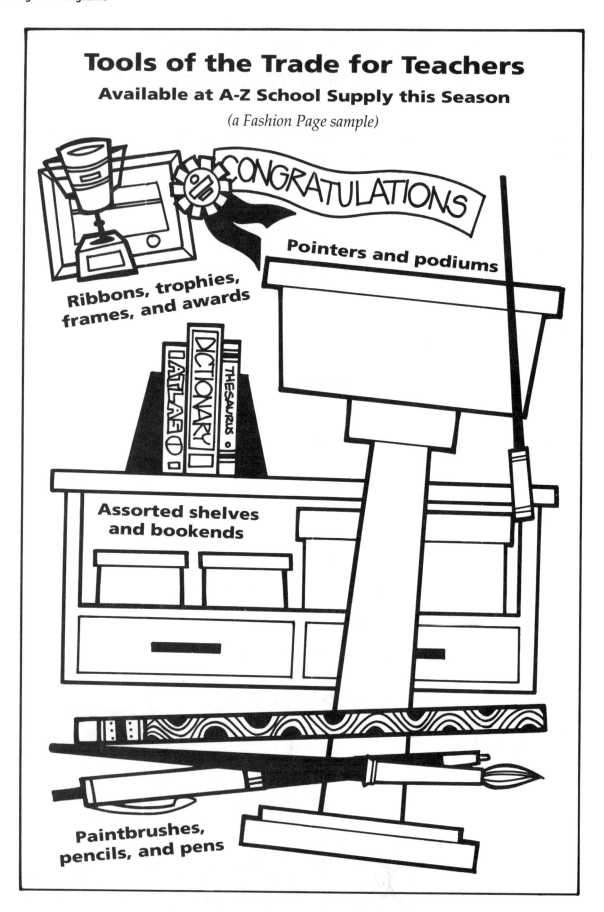

Creating Your Magazine   Name _____

Adding Some Fun: Cartoons, Jokes, Puzzles, and Games

Many magazines include crossword puzzles, riddles, jokes, comics, or games either in a specified section of the periodical or throughout their pages. These "fun" items add *comic relief* and break up traditional layouts to create visual interest. Your group's magazine will include the equivalent of at least two "fun" pages. A one-page social satire and a one-page crossword puzzle might meet this requirement; or you might choose to break up your two pages by adding a political cartoon to your news story, a riddle or two to your poetry page, and a joke at the bottom of pages here and there that are in need of fillers. Answer the questions below, and check out the sample fun page to help you get started.

Fun Page Questions

1. Will your fun page items be contained in a single section of the magazine or will you spread jokes, puzzles, and cartoons throughout your magazine's pages?

   _____

2. Who will write your fun page activities? _____

3. What fun page items and activities will you include (puzzles, games, jokes, comic strips, cartoons, social satires, commentaries, etc.)?

   _____
   _____

4. Which activities will require titles and what will those titles be?

   _____
   _____
   _____

5. Where will you get pictures for your cartoons, puzzles, jokes, or comic strips (student art, clip art, magazines, etc.)?

   _____

6. Will your fun page items relate to the theme of your magazine, or just be entertaining to your magazine's targeted audience?

   _____

Fun Page Sample

DOG CARE WORD SEARCH

```
S T R E L B B I K
G C R A T E I S N
A L E A S H S H W
T O S D I T C O A
D V T B A N U T T
I E X E R C I S E
S T R D Y O T N R
H T A B R U S H G
E N O R A L L O C
S E S N E C I L E
```

BATH   CRATE   LEASH   TRAINING
BED   DISHES   LICENSE TREATS
BISCUITS EXERCISE LOVE   VET
BRUSH   I.D. TAG REST   WATER
COLLAR KIBBLE   TOY

RIDDLE CORNER

Q: When does a dog wear more clothes _ in the winter or in the summer?

A: In the summer! In the winter, he wears a coat; in the summer he wears a coat and pants.

CANINE CODE

Add the vowels to find the names of these unusual dog breeds.

SL__GH_   T_S_   S_NSH_   P_M_   DR_V_R
  4 5   3   4 1   1   5   5 3   2 2

| 1A | 2E | 3I | 4O | 5U |

Creating Your Magazine   Name _____

Designing the Back Cover

The back cover of your magazine may be an ad, a drawing, or an attention-grabbing mini-poster with a slogan or quote relating to your magazine's theme. The back cover should be bold, colorful, and attractive. A visitor at the Magazine Trade Show may find your magazine laying upside-down on your display table after another customer has looked at it, or someone might notice the back cover while glancing over at a person who is reading your magazine. In either case, your magazine's back cover could be the first page your viewer sees. So make it count! Whatever you choose to display on your magazine's back cover should make a reader anxious to flip the pages to see more of your group's quality work.

Consider the following:

1. Will your back cover include a full-page drawing or painting, a clever ad, an illustrated quote or slogan, or some other specified item?
   _____

2. How will your back cover relate to your magazine's theme?
   _____
   _____

3. Who will design your back cover? _____

On separate sheets of paper, create three mock-ups of your back cover. Allow your fellow group members to vote on their favorite idea before you create your magazine's actual back cover.

Creating Your Magazine

Putting It All Together: Placing Articles, Ads, and Extras

Making decisions about just how your magazine will be put together will be a group activity. Although the Word from the Editor and Contributors' Corner are introductory columns that belong at the front of your magazine, other articles can be placed wherever you see fit. Ads and extras should be used to break up the more traditional layout of denser articles.

Remove all documents from your group's "Completed Works" folder and spread them out on a large table or a group of desks that have been pushed together. Arrange the documents in a logical order, and use the following questions to help you identify any changes that might need to be made in your placement of articles, ads, and extras. When your group is satisfied with the order of documents, record your decisions on the following page. Number the pages of your articles and other documents (with the exception of ads and the front and back covers, which will not be numbered nor appear in the Table of Contents). Reserve page number one for your Table of Contents.

1. Is your front cover page first, followed by a blank page reserved for your Table of Contents, your Word from the Editor page, and your Contributors' Corner page?

2. Are ads, fun pages, fashion pages, and/or less dense material used to break up denser articles?

3. Are your Special Report documents together or spread throughout the magazine? Decide with the other members of your group which arrangement works the best.

4. Have you kept the pages of multiple-page articles together whenever possible?

5. Were you able to alternate pages containing pictures and graphs with pages having none?

Creating Your Magazine   Name _____

Recording Your Decisions

On the lines below, record the names of articles and other documents as well as descriptions of ads in the order that they will appear in your magazine. Also list the page number of each to assist you in creating a Table of Contents. (Use another piece of paper if you need more space.)

Document	Page Number
Front Cover	does not apply
Table of Contents	1
	2
(A Word from the Editor)	
	3
(Contributors' Corner)	
Back Cover	does not apply

Create a Magazine
© The Learning Works, Inc.

Creating Your Magazine

Packaging Your Product

Now that you have completed all of the pages of your magazine and decided upon a page order, it is time to package your magazine for others to enjoy and critique. Use the suggestions below to help you complete your Table of Contents, and bind your magazine's pages in a cover.

Be sure your magazine's Table of Contents includes:

1. The title of each article and document in your magazine. For projects that are not readily identified by title, use the project title as a subtitle so that your teacher can grade your magazine easily. For example: "Crime in America—A Special Report Cover Article."
2. Subheadings when appropriate. For example, you may want to use subheadings to list all fun page activities (if they are located in one spot), or all Special Report items.
3. Page numbers that correspond to all documents (with the exception of the front and back covers, advertisements, and/or fun page items).
4. Lots of white space, and pictures or borders to add visual interest.

Your group should decide on a binding method for your magazine. Choose a report folder or binder with a clear cover. You also may want to laminate your pages and/or front and back covers.

Section IV
Evaluating Your Work

Trading Magazines

Congratulations! You and the other members of your group have just created a complete, professional-looking pilot magazine. Before presenting your work at the Magazine Trade Show, you will trade magazines with another group and make and receive suggestions for minor improvements.

Gather with the other members of your group. Trade magazines with the group closest to you. Eventually you will have a chance to evaluate each other's projects with the use of an evaluation form, but for now, just enjoy reading the other group's magazine. Have one student in your group read the magazine's title and cover page information, and then pass the magazine around to all group members for a round-robin reading of articles and ads. Be sure all group members get a chance to see any pictures and diagrams.

Once each group has had a chance to enjoy reading another group's magazine, switch magazines again until all groups have read all magazines. Then get a copy of the Evaluation Form from your teacher, and prepare to more thoroughly review the work of your classmates.

Evaluating Your Work   Name _____

Evaluation Form

Trade magazines with another group so that you and your fellow group members can more thoroughly evaluate the magazine of *one* other group using this form. Your group will need to elect a reader and a secretary. The reader will present articles one at a time and give each group member a chance to see the layout and accompanying graphics. The secretary will record your group's comments on the Evaluation Form (this page and page 70).

1. List your group's positive comments about the magazine overall. Which articles, columns, and graphics are the strongest? Which projects have the best layouts?

   _____
   _____
   _____
   _____
   _____

2. Are all required articles included in the magazine you are evaluating? Does each article meet the specific requirements set forth for it?

   _____
   _____

3. Is the theme of the magazine you are evaluating clearly stated? Do articles, columns, and other projects adhere to the stated theme? Are advertisements directed at an audience that would likely buy a magazine devoted to this theme?

   _____
   _____
   _____

4. Comment on the use of grammar, punctuation, sentence structure, spelling, and general mechanics in the magazine.

   _____
   _____

5. Comment on the clarity and readability of articles. Are articles well written and individual paragraphs and stories clearly organized?

   _____
   _____

Create a Magazine
© The Learning Works, Inc.

Evaluating Your Work   Name _____

Evaluation Form
(continued)

6. Comment on the graphics, illustrations, and layouts of the articles, ads, and extras in the magazine you are evaluating.

   _____
   _____

7. Comment on the packaging of the magazine you are evaluating. Is the Table of Contents clearly presented? Is the binding method effective?

   _____
   _____

8. Make valid and reasonable suggestions for *minor* changes that would improve the magazine you are evaluating:

Article, Ad, or Extra	Page Number	Suggested Change
_____	_____	_____
_____	_____	_____
_____	_____	_____
_____	_____	_____

9. Keeping in mind the theme and strengths of the magazine you are evaluating, make suggestions as to how it could best be marketed at the trade show. What features should be highlighted? What advertising techniques would be successful?

   _____
   _____

Create a Magazine
© The Learning Works, Inc.

Evaluating Your Work

Conducting a Discussion Group

Now that you have had a chance to evaluate another group's magazine, it is time to take a serious look at your own product. The discussion group suggestions and questions that follow will help you and your fellow group members to objectively evaluate your own magazine and to make revision decisions.

1. Elect group members to hold the following positions:

   Reader: The group reader will read aloud the comments from the evaluating group as recorded on the Evaluation Form. He or she will also locate and read any articles or sections of articles referred to on the form.

   Discussion Leader: The group discussion leader will lead your group in answering the Discussion Group Questions (page 72), and in making decisions about revisions.

   Secretary: The group secretary will record members' responses to the Discussion Group Questions.

   Discussion Participants: All other group members will participate in discussions about potential magazine revisions and trade show presentation tactics.

2. Have the group's Reader read aloud the comments of the evaluating group as recorded on the Evaluation Form.

3. Have the Discussion Leader begin a dialogue about your magazine using the questions on page 72.

Evaluating Your Work

Discussion Group Questions

1. In general, do you agree with the positive comments the evaluating group recorded for question #1 of the Evaluation Form? Do you have additional positive remarks to add about your magazine as a whole?

2. Do you agree with the evaluating group's comments regarding your magazine's general use of grammar and mechanics, clarity and readability, success at sticking to the theme and meeting article requirements, use of graphics, and effectiveness of packaging? If not, which comments are not in line with the thoughts of your own group members? Do you have additional comments to add to any of these areas?

3. Is your group interested in making any of the changes suggested by the evaluating group for question #8? If so, which ones? Why are you not interested in making the other suggested changes? Are there additional changes your group would like to make?

4. Will the suggestions made by the evaluating group about how to market your magazine at the trade show (question #9) be helpful? Why or why not? Do you have additional ideas about how to present your magazine at the show? If so, record them here.

Now record your revision decisions on the following two pages.

Evaluating Your Work

Name _____

Revision Decisions

Article, Ad, or Extra	Planned Revision (if any)	Due Date
Front Cover		
Table of Contents		
A Word from the Editor		
Contributors' Corner		
The Mailbox		
Special Report Cover Article		
Special Report Article #1		
Special Report Article #2		
Special Report Chart or Graph		
Profile or Interview		
Short Story or Poetry Page		
New Products Preview		
"A Look Back" or "Future Forward"		
How-To Page		
Voice of the Critic		
Advice Column		

Evaluating Your Work Name _____

Revision Decisions
(continued)

Article, Ad, or Extra	Planned Revision (if any)	Due Date
What's New?		
Essay/Opinion Page		
Advertisement #1		
Advertisement #2		
Advertisement #3		
Advertisement #4		
The Fashion Page		
Fun Page Item #1		
Fun Page Item #2		
Fun Page Item #3		
Fun Page Item #4		
Fun Page Item #5		
Back Cover		
Other: _____		
Other: _____		
Other: _____		

Section V
Sharing Your Creation

Sharing Your Creation

Inviting Guests to the Magazine Trade Show

You and your fellow group members have created a great pilot magazine. It's time to show off your project at the Magazine Trade Show. Other teachers and their classes, school administrators and staff members, parents and other relatives, the media, and members of the larger community are all potential guests for your show. All you have to do is invite them. So discuss with your teacher the best date, time, and place for your big event, and then get the word out using one or more of the methods listed below.

Posters advertising the time and place of the trade show can be hung around your school and your community.

Flyers can be distributed to all students at your school and/or delivered to local business owners who may be willing to post them in their windows.

Newspaper advertisements announcing the trade show and highlighting its date, time, and location can be placed in a school publication, or in your local community newspaper.

Invitations can be sent to parents and others whom you especially wish to attend.

A sample invitation follows; its general content can help guide the creation of posters, flyers, and newspaper ads, as well.

Sharing Your Creation

Sample Invitation

_____'s _____ grade class

_____ School

School Address

Today's Date

Guest's Name and Address

Dear _____ ,

For the past few weeks, our class has been working on the creation of pilot magazines that we will be presenting at a Magazine Trade Show in the _____ of our school from _____
(gym, auditorium, library, etc.) (time)
to _____ on _____ . We would like to invite
(time) (date)
you to visit our trade show to view and evaluate our magazines. In addition to reading our magazines, trade show attendees will be able to view displays, enjoy dramatizations, and watch and listen to audio, video, and live presentations.

We hope you can attend our Magazine Trade Show. We look forward to your evaluations of our pilot magazines.

Sincerely,

_____'s _____ grade class

Sharing Your Creation

Setting Up Your Magazine Display Booth

Whether you hold your Magazine Trade Show in the school gym, library, or some other location, you and your fellow group members will need a large table (or a number of desks pushed together) and some wall space (or a display curtain) to cover with items related to your magazine's theme. Follow the suggestions below to create an exciting and attractive display for your group's pilot magazine.

1. **Use bright colors.** Computer-generated color posters; signs with large, bold, and brightly-colored lettering; streamers; brightly-painted student artwork; and a commercial or homemade table skirt can all add attractive color to your display.

2. **Be conscious of eye-level choices.** Viewers are going to hone in on eye-level information as they are drawn closer to your booth by your decorations and posters. Use a book holder to display your magazine upright and at eye-level. If possible, create more than one color copy of your magazine for display. Have a few black-and-white copies available for times when several visitors arrive at your booth at once.

3. **Don't forget the walls or curtain.** Background posters and lettering should highlight your magazine's title, theme, and individual articles. Short, catchy quotes and phrases can grab attention as well as colorful posters and picture displays.

4. **Make it multimedia.** Include a slide show presentation or display photographs of your group members at work on your magazine. Set up a tape recorder and headphones for customers interested in listening to some of your magazine's articles on audio tape. Play a video presentation of the articles in your magazine. Create live dramatizations of portions of your project. Display standing props behind and along the sides of your table. (See pages 79–84 for more ideas.)

5. **Provide handouts.** Increase the impact of your presentation by providing something for your trade show visitors to take with them. Offer theme-related bookmarks, buttons, business cards, snacks, etc.

6. **Dress the part.** Either wear business-type clothing with a button or sticker that advertises your magazine, or dress in a theme-related costume to attract visitors.

7. **Provide an Evaluation Drop Box.** Visitors will receive several Evaluation Forms as they enter the Magazine Trade Show. Somewhere in your display, provide them with a place to put the forms they have used to evaluate your booth.

Sharing Your Creation

Producing a Televised, Live, or Radio Broadcast Magazine Show

In addition to having magazine props, posters, and handouts in your booth, it would be fun to have a video presentation of your product running in the background or alongside your display table. If a camcorder and VCR are not available for your group to use, your group members can produce a live magazine presentation. Schedule several performances of your presentation during the day. List the performance times on a poster displayed somewhere within your booth.

A televised or live magazine show is not a dramatization of one or more of the stories within your magazine (although including a play or skit that dramatizes one of your articles live or on tape would certainly add to your presentation, as well). Your magazine show will be more like the television shows *60 Minutes* and *Hard Copy*. You and your other group members will become anchor people and reporters. You will introduce your magazine, display production credits, read selected articles, and create transitions between stories.

Rather than creating a live or videotaped presentation of your magazine's articles and ads, your group members may choose to create a radio broadcast by taping your show on audio cassettes for trade show visitors to listen to on headphones. Whichever method you choose, the worksheet, steps, and Magazine Show Line-Up Form which follow will help you get started.

Sharing Your Creation   Name _____

Magazine Show Worksheet

1. Who will anchor your magazine show? _____
2. Who will be your camera person? _____
3. Which articles will be presented in your show? _____
4. Who will report on each article? _____
5. Your magazine show will begin by listing production credits. Use the lines below to list your show's credits.

    Your magazine's title: _____

Articles to be Presented	Article Authors	Article Reporters
_____	_____	_____
_____	_____	_____
_____	_____	_____
_____	_____	_____
_____	_____	_____

    Names of production crew members (director, camera persons, tape recorder operators, artists, hair dressers, etc.):

    _____
    _____
    _____

    Production location and date: _____

6. If you are creating a live or televised show, what props will you need to create a "newsroom" scene and/or other scenes? If you are creating a radio broadcast, what sound effects and/or background music will you add?

    _____
    _____
    _____

Sharing Your Creation   Name _____

Magazine Show Worksheet
(continued)

7. Write an introduction to your magazine show on the lines below. (Get ideas from your magazine's Word from the Editor page.)

   _____
   _____
   _____
   _____
   _____

8. You and your group members will dramatize advertisements from your magazine to create *transitions* between articles. Record here the scripts for three dramatized advertisements:

   Transition One: _____
   _____
   _____
   _____

   Transition Two: _____
   _____
   _____
   _____

   Transition Three: _____
   _____
   _____
   _____

9. Write a conclusion for your magazine show on the lines below.

   _____
   _____
   _____
   _____
   _____

Create a Magazine
© The Learning Works, Inc.

Sharing Your Creation   Name _____

Magazine Show Line-Up Form

Record below the line-up of shows and transitions you have scheduled for your taped or live magazine presentation. Use another piece of paper if you need more room.

Article or Other Segment	Reporter	Props/Set-Up Notes
Title and credits presentation	_____	credits on board or cards
Introduction to show	_____	_____
Article #1: _____	_____	_____
Article #2: _____	_____	_____
Article #3: _____	_____	_____
Transition #1: _____	_____	_____
Article #4: _____	_____	_____
Article #5: _____	_____	_____
Article #6: _____	_____	_____
Transition #2: _____	_____	_____
Article #7: _____	_____	_____
Article #8: _____	_____	_____
Article #9: _____	_____	_____
Show's conclusion _____	_____	_____

Create a Magazine
© The Learning Works, Inc.

Sharing Your Creation

Steps to Producing a Magazine Show

1. Using the Magazine Show Line-Up Form on page 82, create a line-up for the magazine articles you will include in your show

2. Write your magazine show production credits on a note card for a radio broadcast; on cue cards for a live presentation; or on posterboards, a dry erase board, or a chalkboard for the camera person to focus in on for a videotaped show.

3. Gather all props and equipment needed to produce your show.

4. Create the set if you are producing a live or videotaped show. Set up chairs, desks, and a tape recorder and microphones if you are producing a radio broadcast.

5. Whether you are taping your show or performing a live broadcast, first conduct several rehearsals to give you a chance to identify and correct any problems. If you are taping your show, take time to edit out any errors.

6. Begin your show:
   - State the title of your magazine and read, announce, or show the credits.
   - Read the introduction to your magazine show (#7 from page 81).
   - Follow the line-up of shows and transitions you listed on page 82.
   - Read the conclusion to your show (#9 from page 81).

83

Create a Magazine
© The Learning Works, Inc.

Sharing Your Creation

Presenting, Reading, and Demonstrating Article Information

You have created a colorful, multimedia display booth to showcase your pilot magazine; but despite all your preparations, your product cannot sell itself. You and your fellow group members must provide the personal touches, dramatizations, and demonstrations that will turn your booth into an exciting, interactive display that sells magazines. All group members need to dress professionally (or in costume), smile, and be friendly, but each of you can choose between several possible specific display booth duties. Choose one or more of the activities listed below, or create your own list of display booth duties, and record who will be responsible for each job on the Specified Duties page that follows.

1. Greet display booth visitors and distribute buttons, snacks, or other goodies.
2. Set up an advice window where visitors can get their questions answered and can read your magazine's actual Advice Column page.
3. Be a "roving reporter" and interview trade show visitors about their experience at the event. Use a camcorder or tape recorder, if possible.
4. Demonstrate the subject or activity described in your magazine's How-To article.
5. Enact your magazine's short story or news article with other group members.
6. Display, demonstrate, or distribute models of products from your New Products Preview page.
7. Show clips from a movie, play songs from a CD, or read phrases from a book that you reviewed in your magazine.
8. Read poetry, short stories, riddles, or jokes from your magazine.
9. Perform live versions of your magazine ads.
10. Roam the trade show floor advertising your booth by distributing flyers or calling out clever slogans or sales pitches.
11. Provide entertainment related to your magazine's theme, such as singing, dancing, instrumental music, or skits.
12. Entertain children with face painting, or hand them balloons or candies.

Create a Magazine
© The Learning Works, Inc.

Sharing Your Creation   Name _____

Specified Duties

Record below the specific duties of each of your group's members in setting up and tearing down your display booth, as well as their responsibilities during the show.

☐ Name: _____
☐ Booth set-up duties: _____
☐ _____
☐ Responsibilities during the show: _____
☐ _____
☐ Booth tear-down duties: _____
☐ _____

☐ Name: _____
☐ Booth set-up duties: _____
☐ _____
☐ Responsibilities during the show: _____
☐ _____
☐ Booth tear-down duties: _____
☐ _____

☐ Name: _____
☐ Booth set-up duties: _____
☐ _____
☐ Responsibilities during the show: _____
☐ _____
☐ Booth tear-down duties: _____
☐ _____

☐ Name: _____
☐ Booth set-up duties: _____
☐ _____
☐ Responsibilities during the show: _____
☐ _____
☐ Booth tear-down duties: _____
☐ _____

Create a Magazine
© The Learning Works, Inc.

Sharing Your Creation

As guests arrive at your Magazine Trade Show, have people at the door welcome them to the event. Provide each visitor with enough copies of the Product Evaluation Form for them to fill one out for each booth. Cut along the dotted line or cover these instructions with appropriate clip art before making copies of the form for trade show visitors.

Product Evaluation Form

Thank you for joining us at our Magazine Trade Show where we hope to "sell" you our magazine pilot ideas through colorful, multimedia, interactive exhibits. Please wander around the trade show floor, read our magazines, view our displays, and enjoy our live presentations. Each time you stop at a booth, write the name of the magazine displayed at the booth on a new Product Evaluation Form, fill out the form, and drop it into the Evaluation Form Drop Box located at that booth.

Title of magazine _____

Please rate the following on a scale from 1 to 5: 1 meaning you do not agree with the statement at all and 5 meaning you very strongly agree.

1. The magazine's title is displayed prominently at this booth.
2. The magazine's theme is made clear through booth displays and presentations.   1 2 3 4 5
3. The booth's workers are friendly and helpful.   1 2 3 4 5
4. The booth's physical display is appealing (table top displays, backdrop or wall artwork, props, etc.)   1 2 3 4 5
5. Multimedia presentations are effectively used at this booth (videotaped or audiotaped magazine shows, slide shows, background music, etc.)   1 2 3 4 5
6. Live demonstrations, dramatizations, and presentations are effectively used at this booth.   1 2 3 4 5
7. The magazine at this booth is well written.   1 2 3 4 5
8. The magazine at this booth has attractive artwork and an interesting layout.   1 2 3 4 5
9. The magazine at this booth is well displayed with a colorful back and front cover and a prominent position in the booth.   1 2 3 4 5
10. If I were a publisher, I would publish this magazine, or if I were a consumer, I would purchase it.   1 2 3 4 5

General comments about this booth or the magazine presented here: _____

_____

Sharing Your Creation

Making the Most of Your Magazine Experience

After your parents, friends, and community members have enjoyed your presentations and displays, and your trade show exhibits have been taken down, gather together with your magazine group members one more time to discuss what you have learned during this *Create a Magazine* unit.

Here are some possible ways to conduct your group's final meeting:

1. Gather all of the evaluation forms from the Magazine Trade Show that pertain to your group's magazine and discuss the results. How was your magazine and your display rated overall? Do you agree with the public's overall rating? What were some of the specific comments made by visitors to your booth? Do you agree with these comments?

2. Discuss what you enjoyed and did not enjoy about the Magazine Trade Show. Did you like your specific duties? Was your group well organized? What turned out great? What did not turn out as well as you would have liked? What effective displays and demonstrations did you see at other exhibits?

4. Turn in a final copy of your magazine for your teacher to evaluate and/or grade.

5. Discuss with your teacher all the aspects of this project—from cooperating with group members to writing and editing articles, from participating in the show to interpreting evaluation form results. What did you learn from the entire process? What would you do differently next time?

6. Write thank-you letters to trade show participants who worked to make the day a success, including administrators, parents, other teachers, the school secretary and/or librarian, etc.

7. Congratulate each other on a job well done!

Proofreader's Marks

¶   begin a new paragraph

cap or ≡   capitalize a lowercase letter

lc or /   lowercase a capital letter

  delete

∧   insert

insert space

◡   close up; delete space

⊐   move right

⊏   move left

⊓   move up

⊔   move down

⊐⊏   center

‖   align vertically

⋏   insert a comma

˅   insert an apostrophe

˅ ˅   insert quotation marks

⊙   change the existing punctuation mark to a period; insert a period

sp   spell out (a number or abbreviation); verify and/or correct spelling

stet   let it stand without making the indicated change or correction

tr or ⊔⊓   transpose

¶ Proof reading is a tedius sp task, a proofreader must carefully compare type set material with the original MS sp to see if the compositer sp has "followed copy." He or she must also determine if the correct type face, size, and weight have been used and if the column width matches the specs sp. These things can only be determined by loking carefully at the designer's and editors marks on the edited manuscript.

Create a Magazine
© The Learning Works, Inc.